BEFORE RAIN

For my parents
Matt and Nancy Reidy

Ger Reidy

BEFORE RAIN

ARLEN
HOUSE

Before Rain

is published in 2015 by
ARLEN HOUSE
42 Grange Abbey Road
Baldoyle
Dublin 13
Ireland
Phone/Fax: 353 86 8207617
Email: arlenhouse@gmail.com
arlenhouse.blogspot.com

Distributed internationally by
SYRACUSE UNIVERSITY PRESS
621 Skytop Road, Suite 110
Syracuse, NY 13244–5290
Phone: 315–443–5534/Fax: 315–443–5545
Email: supress@syr.edu

978–1–85132–125–4, paperback

Typesetting by Arlen House
Printed lithographically in Dublin
Cover paintings by Dermot Seymour
are reproduced by permission of the artist
www.dermotseymour.com

CONTENTS

Acknowledgements

Some of these poems have been published in *The Irish Times, Poetry Ireland Review, Sunday Tribune, The Moth, Cyphers, The SHOp, Force 10, Cathair Na Mart* (historical journal) and have been broadcast on *Sunday Miscellany*. Many of these poems have also been read on local radio, and appeared in the local press.

In thanking people I would like to mention the following: the Arts Council for the granting of a bursary in literature, the Tyrone Guthrie Centre, the late Dermot Healy, Mayo County Council, The Heinrich Böll Committee, the Linenhall Arts Centre, Ian Wieczorek and all my friends who supported me in this publication.

The publisher gratefully thanks Dermot Seymour for his wonderful cover artwork.

Before Rain

LAMENT FOR THE CATTLE JOBBER'S DAUGHTER

Not for you Cinderella's slipper story at bedtime,
only boots to feed the sheepdog with butchers' shins.

Not for you the brush of mother's rouge in the mirror,
only the slap across the face of a cow's wet tail.

Not for you the speckled colours on the dance hall ceiling,
only the torch light loading heifers at Ballinrobe mart.

Not for you the glamour of *Cosmopolitan*,
only *Old Moors Almanac* on the dashboard of the lorry.

Not for you the pink cards of wedding invitations,
only the blue cards of bovine tuberculosis.

Not for you a dry house overlooking the farm,
only a new slatted shed beside the barn.

Not for you roses from a husband on your birthday,
only a bouquet of ragwort on bonfire night.

Not for you Lucozade around the hospital bed,
only a flagon of cider found beside you in the heather,

the sky lark requiem overhead.

The Gift
For Eleanor

Stunned by the joy and terror of a new pulse surging,
hostage to your breathing in a midnight cot
or the pain waiting with childhood as an alibi.
What did we know of the prize
that would make us human and keep delivering,
insisting on throwing colour recklessly everywhere.
The street too had to learn fast that your discoveries
would ignite the tired and renew.
You must have been the earth rod
for the blue music of silence that descends
when two people are abandoned together
in a flat of gas heaters and condensation
facing north where red brick factories
clung to the echo of forgotten workers.
Where a thin garden grew rank weeds,
crowding flowers out beside the disused railway.
The old photos show you trying to be sure footed
on our shifting sands, which rips the heart
before I was visited by the old turbulence
which flung us on to the high road.
But you threw back some forgotten love
which must have overflowed
to bandage the ancient wounds
and set us all going again, laughing at ourselves
with something approaching joy.
Living life like some kind of prayer
in gratitude for the gift of ordinary existence.

SUPPORTERS

They come in waves towards me, short-sleeved,
hairy-armed, pulling children, the hay saved.
The roar of the crowd fills their ropey veins
from townlands and half-parishes,
from an early Mass and the cows milked,
they leave the pitch, fists clenched, triumphant.

Soon mountain winds and seagull echoes gather
through the concrete post and barbed wire while
high-heeled girls pull country boys behind the toilets,
the streets throb as a dog howls in the valley,
the bogs, the streams, the trees are lonely for their return.
They park facing home.

The Awakening
After Patrick Kavanagh

I caught the stray ass in an overgrown quarry,
pulled the blinkers over his lugs and steered him
home, then collar and hames, float over the straddle
five loose links each side and the belly band,
down to the stony field, cart abandoned again.
After he ploughed out the drills of potatoes
I tied him to a bush where he ate weeds at a headland.
We picked Kerr's Pink coated in sleet into warped buckets.

Soon the hills were whitened as the light faded,
we loaded up the cart with torn jute sacks
and whipped him home as a huge moon rose.
The shed floor was covered with old *Woman's Ways*.
On the back pages the colour advertisement for tights,
three girls, two looking away, I never knew where.
Hold the ass straight, my father demanded as the
wet spuds covered the beautiful legs with clay.

GARAGE OFFICE

A sick light from bright spells and showers
fleets across torn invoices
thumb-tacked into the bathroom door.
The oil filter for the Volvo truck
lies beside the gas heater –
it's the wrong model, but they won't take it back.

Sometimes between phone calls
Bernie looks out the oily window
beyond the heap of crashed cars
at the stream where she bathes her feet.
It tells her about last night's rain.
Soon she will drive the van that says

break-down service available day and night,
to collect a fire-log and briquettes
to arrive at a rented flat over the butcher's
where she greets little Kylie
and lets the sitter go into the night,
she too advocating brake pads and exhausts.

ONE MORNING IN MAY

Early morning we cut the engine
and drift as clouds going nowhere
bloom over the hills.
Spinning off the rocks
they coil on every hook,
gasping together in a fetor.

The boat man guts some,
eyes incredulous as the knife rips –
'They'd be lovely on the grill for lunch,
I filled the freezer with them last year'.
As he speeds off into another day
the bag of mackerel form a dumb mass.

I am reminded on the pier
as they writhe against my leg.

I am jolted in the car
as they thresh across the seat.

I am haunted in my sleep
as they swim into my brain.

THE TURNING

Already the great chariot turns towards winter,
the horses demand respite
but Time's tyrant lashes the whip.
The lost boy called from the beach
has heard that sound old men fear
and pursues the team in vain.

Gather your children before it's too late,
you who stand at the water's edge,
distract them with ice-cream and funfairs,
let them not smell the harness sweat
or see the flared nostrils equinox-bound
or the backward glance of the charioteer.

A Death in Winter

Fox howl pierces through sleety winds
as I scan the ditches for a missing ewe,
when the torch finds the biblical eyes
I am witness to the private miracle.

Still assaulted by the elemental
where one is dead and one alive,
I must play my part in the dumb ceremony.
She stomps her foot trailing the afterbirth

as I throw the dead one over my shoulder
and limp towards the shining hayshed.
A half moon is released from clouds
and begins to reign over a whiter landscape.

As I close the gate against her bleating
I mutter something before the lights go out
and retreat into the foetal position,
that one heartbeat cannot assume the next.

THE DAY FALLS OPEN

The day falls open, I enter –
the only boundaries are darkness,
for a while only wind and cold sunshine.
Soon come the leathery chords
of guitars from the high plateau.
Like the sky, my day fills with people, words
and the cloying servitude of flesh.
The clouds gather for the day's storm
as if they're discovering weather.
After the drops start to fall,
there can only be one ending.

Silence

After the bomb went off on Bridge Street
we nodded and winked our right to say nothing.
Some say it came from the colonised South
where words went underground.

We excel when a great tragedy
occurs on some remote shore,
our leaders donate a full minute,
while time wanders among us with a leer.

The Monet glow of childhood
was scarred and I withdrew when
father's words came out wrong,
and mother wouldn't talk for a week.

When the Hereford cow strayed into Maguire's
Meadow it took a generation to break,
sometimes we discover a silence without peace
tears into a scream and then a gun.

THE INSIDE ROOM

Don't let the stray dogs saunter through,
or the friends, with only their patio doors open.
Stop the siblings who can't open theirs
and your parents who think they squat inside,
deflect the boys, who want to dump your furniture
and the old men, who have lost their key.

Above all avoid the cloying fires of intimate strangers.
The opening will happen when no one is looking,
like the desert flower when least expected.
For it can be opened only from inside,
after which it can never be closed against
the herds, the armies, the indifferent lovers.

ECHOES AT ROSMONEY

You knew the whine of the wind at the point,
the yachts' tinkle in a fresh breeze,
the roar of the swell before a storm,
the sand bars that weren't on any chart,

the spring current that carries the stones,
how to scan the clouds for showers,
the psychic knowledge of boat engines,
ancestral knots that couldn't be learnt,

the casual precision of the perfect landing.
Now although you're gone you're everywhere.
All I see is the soft beam of your modest smile
looking up at me on a summer morning,

warning me that the steps are slippery
and that every year the sea takes its own.
Those words now echo from island to island
never to make landfall.

MAROONED

A day borrowed or remaindered from youth,
the tide gone out, the sea in the distance,
when we adored girls, drank wine and fell asleep.
We would be at the centre of it all soon enough.

I awake now to the deafening ocean,
alone, waves surround me,
my friends huddle on their own sandbars.
The water too deep now, memories lap at my feet.

Far off my son sleeps unaware on a grassy mound,
beside me my father's bones are polishing the rocks.

THE RECKONING

After thirty seven years in revenue
our boss had to travel to the island.
He kissed his wife and girls goodbye
and clutched the tax file in the cabin.

After he met the drift net fishermen
he issued them with a bill and went to bed early.
All night he swooned to the heave of the swell
on the beach outside his window.

On the way back to the office
he stood on the prow smiling at the waves.
Then he tore page after page from the file
and let the wind take it into the slipstream.

He laughed louder, shouting at the ocean
our boss getting all wet, tie missing,
slowly becoming beautiful and useless.
What will we do with him?

Departures

You find yourself in a ringside seat
holding a boy on a dual carriageway,
the blue lights' arrival futile.
The ultimate scream into the sky
as the mother discovers him,
or on the train as a wife runs alongside
the emigrant beside you, weeping.

Until that day you earn the ticket
and the pulse quickens from finite hours
as you examine the positive results,
and your loved ones become strangers
mouthing the necessary language
as useless as the intercom words in your ears
wash your hands with the soap provided.

BEFORE RAIN

Foreboding roamed the desolate streets
as if a wild animal had been cut loose,
country people talked of a strange storm,
a string quartet ran off the bandstand,
sixty-seven bikers turned into the square,
a woman flicked open a pink mirror.

Frightened traders gave away shirts,
a forgotten language entered mouths,
dispatches were received from upwind,
somebody sang *A Whiter Shade Of Pale*,
Stravinsky swung a glass pickaxe in my head.
This happened one day before the sky opened.

After Rain

Coming home that Sunday evening after the long drive,
we passed an old house under a low hill.
The blue smoke urged itself sideways
into a sky opening like a stage.

A chainsaw was wrecking the silence far away.
The fat man with the white coat passed by on a Honda 50.
A new season had declared itself,
something cold and beautiful was happening.

THE BETRAYAL

Who can remember now the evenings we threw away,
when the sun couldn't go down,
and we absorbed the bounty of contentment
as it leaked through our clutching hands.

Now the wind whistles through rib cages
as I gather the corpses in a flooded field
and drag them, their dirty trails meeting
where the greybacks gather.

Others watch, beyond life, where they know,
curiosity redundant, everything finally clear,
nailing daily into my soul the stains of neglect
with the betrayed innocence of their grassy dreams.

AT DUSK

At dusk a man came running out of the woods
into the city, chasing a wild boar.
Look, he shouted, there, his hoof marks.
We all ran around looking for him,
the animal extinct since the famine.

The man ran back into the woods before dawn,
the city razed to the ground, looking for a pig.
When I told my father this story
he looked out the window of the train
for a long time into the night.

COME AND SEE
after Klimov

Every village has that day when blood sluices.
The typical morning where mums and dads rush,
but soon the men are taken.

The women leave for the woods in single file
while the children stay in school, unaware.
Only the idiot and the cows remain.

At midday a fog from the east blows through.
At dusk the soldiers leave, taking hens and a pig,
leaving only a girl walking spread-legged.
The partisans arrive under the moonlight.

THE CRACKED YARD

The girl tiptoes across the canal bridge
where little black waves
nudge against a floating car bonnet,
high heels keep her safely
beyond school mums and office girls,
resting for a while at the roundabout,
unaware, using a cigarette as a prop
while gazing across the river.

She remembers the old country
and the smell of cow dung and semen
in the hay barn after an uncle
left the impression they shared.
How her father agreed to accept a school fee,
how sunlight crept along the gables
and insinuated itself into the bedroom
caressing as the tears leaked.

But now it's dark and the cars circle,
looking away, nobody can touch her.
Choosing old men – tobacco and sweat –
as a bachelor's van fogs up in the alley,
she holds him desperately close
to smell that old hay barn in his jacket,
to see the harvest sunlight flooding
into that cracked yard all afternoon.

BEING

After a night of calm steady rain
this day lies before me prostrate,
dripping with expectation,
like gazing through an ancient gate
across a collective farm
spreading to the faint blue horizon.
Overwhelmed I want to fill it
with the furniture of living,
but instead I hear
awareness trickling into the voids.

Events: the sound of junk mail in the hall,
soot falling across the floor at noon,
shadows lengthening again
until the evening is quietly defeated
above the murmuring ocean.
If I could divert the static of my existence
and feel time passing,
maybe I could learn to celebrate
the eternity of remaining days,
and fall gently into being.

THE SORCERER

Before the master bolted the heavy door
and the rainy holidays descended,
the gypsy girl brushed past him
to spin the world and then she laughed.
It stopped and Cuba faced out against the stars.
As he closed the iron gate
the call of children echoed in the classroom
before the gulls swooped to the playground

All summer the moonlight crept across the desks
and stole as far as the breast pocket
of the master's threadbare waistcoat
where they discovered a señorita's photo.
A mouse stirred twice behind a skirting board.
Only the hurricanes came across the Atlantic that August
and when the school opened Señor O'Shea was missing.
The girl smiled up at Sister Brid, and spun the globe again.

DAUGHTERS

They bloomed after we shared tea
and laughter with their mother.
As she drives off I walk into the garden.

Separated, they tease me about girlfriends
before wandering down the lane giggling,
towards the village for ice cream.

Leaves drift in a warm breeze.
I lean on the same gate as my father did,
and then it occurs to me –

as their voices fade beyond a turn
I am at the centre of a memory
that is not over yet.

THE LIMINALS

Perched on a grassy knoll outside the fence
the discarded souls rest, remote,
on a wedge of rock hanging
– they didn't receive the blessing.

Below the ocean gouges out, relentlessly
like a mindless zombie undermining
with its arm around time, it can wait
for the prize of bones on the shore.

Suspended and unresolved
they taunt us, refuse to be forgotten,
their limboed dismissal mocks our gait.
They beckon us to cross the rope bridge .

On still nights they stroll among us
as the white night defines Mweelrea,
moon rays choosing their granite stones
blast gold flecks into our earthly lives.

ELEMENTAL

The landscape darkened, the features quenched,
the sky looms with the maw of the ocean,
mountains conjure up November rains,
people scurry, not knowing what's out there.

The gaunt ash on the horizon are waiting,
lights extinguish in the distance,
the games of the fox and the hare are eclipsed,
ships succumb to tired harbours.

Premonition floods the burrows of the sensitive,
summer's gifts are stored in roots and memories,
soon the islands receive the signal,
then everything is subjected to the elemental.

DEEP WATER

We row out from the city on the black river
beyond the streetlights to the estuary,
gleaning sounds from the dark,
avoiding the shallows in search of deep water
where we cast the net and wait.

Some nights we get pulled out to sea
by a psychotic creature from the depths
and lose sight of what we are to each other.
Most dawns one of us swims ashore
so we can laugh at ourselves over dinner.

Having drunk from the rolling ocean
we are condemned never to fish in safe pools.
But on my way home some mornings
I walk through children and tame ducks
as they reserve a place in a family photograph.

THE INVERSION

You keep falling at a terminal speed through nets,
concrete floors, days and years,
through families, friends, elations, depressions.
You wake up falling, you go to sleep falling
until falling becomes your second name.
You fall through the sky,
you fall through women who want to fall with you,
fall through history and wars,
through reeks of pleading corpses
until living seems like falling.
Then you fall through living,
before you fall through dying.
You forget to stop falling.
You fall through time, the universe
until one morning after you check out
of a cheap hotel in another city you look up
to see the poplars bend and sing
in a strange wind from snowy mountains.
Turned upside down you rise through everything.

Autobiography

When the darkness came to our village
it rattled our doors and sucked from our chimneys.
People held each other until the turmoil ceased,
until their love shivered with reassurance.
It found its victim on the margins and assumed her.

I was singing a song from a forgotten war,
chewing a wisp in the meadow, oblivious.
She joined me from across the border,
her blue bridal hand in mine.

THE MIDDAY TRAIN

One day I had to leave
my aunt to the station,
make sure to wear a black tie,
can't wait to see mum and dad, she said.

It will be soon now, said Fr Quinn.
I have the golf clubs packed,
the fourteenth takes a six iron,
I kissed my aunt and waved.

Everywhere there were country men
chatting about the price of store cattle.
I asked a drunken woman why it was late.
I've been waiting here for years, she said.

I can never get a seat, that's life,
some babies don't get off at all
and others, mostly young men,
get on without a ticket.

It's always late on a Tuesday,
something to do with the hospital.
Looking up into me, she said,
I hate standing on the train, don't you?

END GAME

Disconnected, the human race another species,
you ride into town on the last sunny day,
tie your horse outside Supavalu,
wandering like a broken king.

The Black Queen is waiting at the town clock
peering down the chessboard of streets.
You're the only one who can see her.
She knows your move and whispers it into your ear.

She swoops down the diagonal to the square
to squint at her prey from another angle
and measure the pensioners scurrying to Mass.
The Bishop can't protect them now.

She glides along the river,
arrives back at the clock and settles her robe.
In the dead of night her eyes light up as she ascends
with a pawn in each claw, the day's bounty.

THE SUNDAY DRIVE

That summer on our Sunday drive
with children and grandmother,
suddenly we came to a place
where the trees swung violently,
the village desolate, the river dry,
overhead crows circled,
clouds swooped down to clutch the mountains.
We drove hard and straight but couldn't escape.
A church bell rang as we turned and fled.
Crowds appeared in the rear view mirror.

EXISTENCE

Yesterday's leaking pathos
infects the fledgling day
as it struggles to forge a morning
like your first lover haunts
a new date with parody.

But the demise of passion
never vaccinates us against it,
so we clamber out of bed
somewhere in the tangled city
with that intimate half-awake gesture.

We must draw the torn curtains,
invoking the frail dawn,
filtered through yellowed glass,
to play on us whatever tune it can,
shattering light into a new existence.

The Inspection

When she knew who I was her eyes started dancing.
'Look, it's Matt's son, remember my boss I talked about
from the factory when we were courting
after all these years', she held her husband close,
showed me all her family photographs.
'Sit down', she demanded.
Her family entered the room,
the table set, the fire glowing.

'He looks exactly like him – the nose, the chin'.
Up a country lane, big tractors parked outside, I found him,
here, he was at the head of the table.
This is how we go on,
in the rushed display of eggs and cheese
in the fuss of a grandmother on a wintry afternoon
in the pause for silence before we break bread
in the grace falling like dew after.

GALE WARNING

On western shores the feeble sun
is reaped into the ocean
by sickles of thunderous cloud.
Mountainous waves rush in
with the news to the calm bay,
gently warning the quieter inlets.
The widow pauses, and runs
when she hears the roar at the headland.

To the east the blue night
grows from a tranquil sea
while an awesome moon appears.
Embraced by Georgian crescents
yachts chuckle in the marina.
A fisherman's wife looks out to sea,
feels a sudden breeze on her face,
and worries at her wedding ring.

IN THE AFTERNOON

Where the women gather in the afternoon
the builders replace the water pipes,
children play games in the cold sunshine,
a sudden breeze ushers a flurry of leaves.
The war veteran in a wheelchair comes to watch,
eyes hook through alleyways, no one escapes.
Upstairs the baby is displaced for a while.
Conchita gazes at the poster of La Paz while waiting,
soon she is feeding her little boy
before descending to the street.
The wind is coming off the mountains,
old men stare from park seats.

GULL

Why are you here in the dunes
looking sideways at me?
I turn you again in hope, only
to admire the cold perfection.
Decorated for flight, nothing surplus
except the split second hesitancy
a Formula One driver might encounter
in a twitching dream
but too much for nature
which gave you the chequered flag.

What are you doing here?
I turn you again to wonder at
the undercarriage tucked away,
tail gathered at the ready.
A lonely gull banks close by, waiting.
What charges through your mind, looking up
at the fleeting clouds through marram grass,
what narrow comfort from a clumsy alien
as your eye rolls back
like the bubble on a spirit level?

THE MISTRESS

I have left her waiting all these years
trawling through forsaken towns,
gleaning the essence of port cities,
scouring mountain tops in winter,
in vain looking for her,
when all the time she was at home.
I come here when there's nowhere left to go.

She still smiles when I fall in the door.
Oozing across the rooms at night
she dances with me through generations,
she becomes every woman I could know
while the ancestors applaud.
In the morning strange words
are found written on torn paper.

EXPOSURE

Gather the weeping silences
from those sepiaed childhood holidays
with a pitch fork reserved for still births.
Hang them on a gnarled bush facing north,
planted in winter by your dead mother.

Here the grey crows will gorge themselves
until there is nothing left but the rhetoric
that you wear as a mask,
until your first love tears it off
and the whole thing starts again.

GHOST TOWN

Up here only wind,
it plays its ceaseless war with stone,
exploits a stray cloud in a timeless plot
to create useless floods, enough to suggest life.

I have seen dried bones beside the mine
and heard the Spanish bell in the ruins.
Love passed through once
and squandered blood on the rocks.

Even here there were red torrents
to satisfy the blind gale
condemned to weep for itself as it whines
through the tangled afterbirth of history.

HIS AND HERS

Wire tied between gnarled bushes
hacked each year with a bow saw,
faithfully they grow through metal and nails.
Timber clothes' pegs, springs rusted
hold something that once was
a child's pink sock, a Spice Girls t-shirt,
an Offaly jersey. There too on the other side,
long Johns, yellowed, elastic gone,
hers faithfully beside, both dripping,
discoloured in sympathy.
They all swing in unison
in that last gentle breeze
before frost in late January
near the main road
between Galway and Dublin.

GENERATIONS

When that warped hammer
discovered by your grandfather
falls into the long grass, try not to find it
when fencing with your son
he will keep looking, always seeing it
as some kind of loss.
He too will have explaining to do
when it gets caught up in the mowing machine.
As he relays the story to his grandchildren,
he might finally understand why the handle
was painted green, firing it over his shoulder
after giving it a fresh coat of gloss.

IN A ROADSIDE COTTAGE

As winter fell they watched the rain,
wave upon wave sink into their words
its weight lodged between them
until, on the solstice, speech failed.

One morning when all seemed lost
the sky blackened to the horizon.
Out of that darkness came snow,
at first hesitant flurries.

Her tentative words fell out,
they resonated in his breastbone,
shuddered in his ribcage,
until his being was purged.

Soon his heartstrings
squeezed an overture, inaudible.
As I passed their roadside cottage
my sheepdog tilted his head,

when he heard the music beyond silence.
I felt the grace bestowed
on the shivering mortals,
distilled from the void of pain.

THE NIGHT BOAT

When my darkness met your winter
we scurried into the ravine
to indulge in reckless games.
After we emerged as a hideous couple
displaying the cracked smiles
of a Goya, it was too late.

Now with our sails filled by a north wind,
we are immune to love.
We drift on a thin sea of parody,
without direction, on a moonless night.
Our proud raft beached on a rocky island,
we wait at the shoreline for dawn.

Shallow waves caress our feet,
we see nothing, we say nothing,
we listen only for a sound
to muffle the whine of the gale
howling through the abandoned gantries
of our forsaken childhood.

INARTICULATE PRAISE

A last sunray sears
through a frond of high cloud
over the sleeping fields.
The moon lurks between
the hay shed and a gable
squinting through a whitethorn bush.

I feel chosen and mumble
inarticulate praise
until the sky is brightening.
To feel this, to be aware
to be here is enough,
present in the forging.

ON THE HORIZON

The sea will never meet the sky
you keep saying, like you and I,
even when the storms
bend down to comb the waves
and the water is sucked into the heavens.

On summer days the distance is unbearable
which is why huge clouds gather and weep.
On clear nights the great jewels
wait in vain for consummation.
But on hopeless afternoons, who knows

what happens out there on the horizon
where that age-old love affair
subjects us mortals to weather,
and vast oceans are swept up
into the arms of simple breezes?

ISLAND FUNERAL

They came through a dawn fog,
the black currach and a flotilla,
the coffin carried along the pier
to a rusty tractor waiting
and a procession across the sand
from houses left in silence.

Some stand, others with cap on knee
and more sit with child,
all held by a song from the altar
blessed by that random light
thrown across the hall
as showers cruised over the bay.

Outside some look towards the mainland
where the last snow is hidden,
others wondered if it is time to set the pots.
At the grave the priest nods and turns away
the pebbles fall like the first drops in a storm
before it settles into that dumb echo

which rips the heart of every man.
The crowd leaks back into the hills
leaving only the angularity of elbow and knee
as wiry men silhouetted heap the daub.
They watch as her only son walks away
into the evening of his life.

THE PETITION

Let me die before the sodium lights
of suburbia reach my townland,
before the whirr of lawnmowers
sunders that primal peace.

Send wintry showers in May
to cleanse this pretty seaside town
to a blue as pure as the tongue
of a perished mountain lamb.

Let polar winds plunge
into the manicured gardens
to thresh the silly cherry blossoms
while the stoic ash looks on.

In old age let me stumble down
the centre of my overgrown lane
assaulted by the smell of woodbine,
like a schoolboy dawdling home

falling asleep under the last oak,
wakening to climb a rusty gate
into a field spreading to the horizon,
lost in the embrace of wild grasses.

JOHN JOE'S LULLABY

Where I went at weekends to forget
they all sang along with John Joe,
'I shot a man in Reno just to watch him die'.
One night he held the wobbly head of a French girl
in a flooded drain as her father whispered
'je t'aime' from the rushy field
and the cow, with mild curiosity,
swivelled her huge ears forward briefly
as she watched the headlights beaming into the sky.

JJ doesn't sing much anymore but he did whisper back
on the girl's behalf before closing her eyes
some broken French he learned from Mrs Geraghty
the year before he started welding in Conroy's garage.

LA MER

Up our way it was your man Debussy
that caused all the bother.
The Co-op threw in a free CD
in the closing down sale with every chainsaw.
John Joe put his on one night
when our parish won the county final.
After twelve tins of Polish beer
he took off, heading for the sea – some say
he went through bushes and barbed wire.
Mrs McGuire met him on her way to t'ai chi
smiling, all raw and wide-eyed.

It was still playing a month after
when the brother heard it coming across the bog
one frosty night, the house still lit up.
Condemned to wander he crossed over too –
water on the brain, the doctor said.
The neighbours afraid to enter, sent the priest.
Every morning they still comb the shoreline.
It was a funny old place – that Co-op, I mean.

The Four Seasons

They put the lame boy in goal,
not because he was left-handed
or had developed a stutter in school,
but his mother had a funny name.

In winter if he let a goal past,
the captain John Joe would slowly
carry him to the dirty pond
in the middle of the pitch and drop him.

In summer he would dump him
in the rank nettles behind the dry toilets.
In spring he would threaten to take his clothes
off in front of the prompting girls.

In autumn he would take out his penknife
and demand they cut the stones out of him.
JJ fell off a scaffolding in Camden Town.
The boy's garden is full of weeds and floods.

MIDWINTER
for Dermot Healy

After months of gales we had lost hope,
when from nowhere a calm day
was bestowed by the gods.
We sailed between islands without words,
except to repeat a mindless refrain
infused with gratitude and redemption.

On one leg the heron stared at his reflection.
Somebody mentioned peace.
The curlew became uneasy, saw something
beyond the lighthouse calling us,
cracked the silence as he flew away.

Then the boat shuddered,
a vortex of angry clouds descended,
the swell gathered on the horizon
throwing us back to the pier
to drive alone into evening traffic, changed.

NOCTURNE

I turn the dial in the dark.
Outside the frost and the moon
embalm from their austere thrones.
Everywhere people are rising,
pointing themselves at the day.
The blinking radio tells me that
someone scored four birdies in Dubai
and shares in Asia are up in early trading.
I fling a hand again to kill the pain,
to hear that a dog is lost in Swinford.
For a long time I listen to the details
and I am half bitten in a childhood dream
delivering the *Far East* to Mrs McGuire.
Again I flake out to twist the groove
when through the static I arrive
at a silence before the first notes fall
that justifies hearing itself.
That makes the world safe again.

Mirror Man

He drinks under a roadside bush
and wears a yellow jacket.
He fights with himself in the park
and scatters the children.

He follows the town parade on the tractor,
sunders groups of middle-aged women,
wears wellingtons in the front row at Mass.
I am the sheriff of Colorado, he announces.

Without a coat in the rain,
with teenagers at the disco,
he indulges in the gentle art of dying.
It becomes the beautiful vocation.

At a burial in winter he observes like a crow
perched beyond rescue with nothing to lose.
We have given him the power
to confront us with the mirror.

OLDER

We grew up between the bog and the mountain,
then one day I encountered the sea.
I said goodbye to my family. Nothing was ever the same.

When I met her we listened at night time
beside the shore. It sang a libretto in the moonlight,
by day a constant symphony.

Now I live on a salt-swept headland
with my back to the noise of the ocean,
my beautiful wife too has become invisible.

MY VILLAGE

It gave me the great afternoon vacancy
and church bells to eulogise the day.

It threw skulls at me to play with
in the long grass on bonfire evening.

It gave me confetti, coffins
and tramps fighting on sheep fair days.

It presented me with the trophy of betrayal
which I accepted as initiation.

Everywhere it played for me
the arid chaconne of crude indifference.

It gave me desolate showers from the hills
tearing across blind lakes.

It robbed from me its gift of nothing.
My village gave me everything.

NETTLES ON THE BALLINROBE ROAD

At a sub-committee meeting
of the Tidy Towns Committee –
all the litter bins freshly painted,
the hanging baskets smothered with colour –
we would surely gain some points.

In another pretty town they're cleansing too,
they throw children on the fire,
but they won't burn
even with petrol and tyres,
so they use mothers instead.

Over to you, smile the brittle ladies.
Item 6D – nettles on the Ballinrobe Road.

THE BUSH REQUIEM

The woman I'll never meet
came strolling at dusk through wet rushes.
She never asked me the question
as she lay beside me and we watched the showers
stalk the horizon before the mountains
were embalmed with snow.
I told her the dead woke me with nocturnes.

In the full moon I visited rocks,
the hares ran away into ditches,
only the bushes in winter spoke to me.
Our shadows played in a fort
before the gale summoned them
to perform a requiem in a minor key.
I was embraced by their thorny branches.

OFFICE BOUND

Late for work I turn a bend
and before me, a family on the open road.
She reprimands them as they dive into a ditch
but the last one is almost caught on my tyre,
I check in the mirror for feathers.
I turn up Hendrix to congratulate myself
but then as suburbia swallows me
I want to feel their warmth.

I return to where I hear a frantic calling,
peer into the water to see mother
swimming away with the others
and there, beside me, the chick suspended on a briar.
Chosen to be a god on a wet morning I reunite them
and watch as they paddle away into a dirty drain.
When I think about this my life makes no sense.

PILGRIMAGE

Fall into the crooked light of a new year
where the ocean throws wild clouds across the sky
and a child cries outside a discount store.

Crawl towards another day of haunted memories
where a schoolboy kicks a beer tin through the docks
and the old skipper falls asleep looking out to sea.

Stumble onto the empty streets of a neglected town,
button your jacket against the January wind
as the black river torrents through gardens.

Hobble into the embrace of a broken woman
who asks where do the lost years go?
She has been waiting to treat you like a king.

THE ANARCHIST

I found him in town for the day,
descended from the mountain valley,
just stepped off the Connemara bus.
On the finest summer day
he has chosen to walk the streets,
eat his sandwiches in the park
and gape at the women.

What are they to do with him,
the residents of Mountain View,
this man in boots and raincoat
who takes long strides and looks at the sky,
who buys nothing?
Mothers will sleep easier when he goes
back to wherever he came from.

RIGA PAINTING

Tied up in the cobbled square
beside melting snow reeks,
everybody had suddenly gone.
He heard a noise down by the pier,
strange with the fields waiting to be here.
His ears pricked forward, relaxed again
as new sunlight rested on his back.

How could he know that his heavy sigh
was a punctuation between epochs,
his breath formed a question mark
insinuating into the middle distance, disappearing.
The little hills were singing in the last sun rays
bathing in the moonlight, but the villages had emptied.
By morning the plough unhooked, replaced with a cannon.

SPRING

It arrives with a parade of afterbirths
and sleet hissing though gorse
where the first primroses are discovered.
The crow gleans in a rusty trough
what the sheep's tongue can't reach
and the fox leaves only the legs behind
for the ewe to find when grazing
with her remaining lamb,
strong and indifferent.

It bursts forth with all the style
of a drunk returning at Christmas
with bailing twine around his suitcase,
a picture of the mistress in his inside pocket
and a broken doll for his daughter.
It emerges with the panache of a baby
whose mother spends her allowance on drink
as she smokes in a high-rise stairwell
watching late snow gather on a bank of rubble.

Then one day it's here.
When did the grass grow so tall,
see the animals sprawled in the heat
and the whitethorn in reckless display?
Where did the wind go, look,
the drunk presenting the girl
with flowers from a cracked pavement
as he wheels their restless baby into town,
echoes of their laughter evaporating?

The Lost Seed

All night her single voice wailing out at sea.
When it made landfall it seeped through the house
as the winter gale deepened.
Hiding was useless, it flung the doors wide.
Desolation prised him open
on the gold table of sacrifice.
That dawn the first sunray entered the ribcage
igniting the lost seed.
He was chosen to become the host
to a cluster of evocations.

THE SMALL CEREMONY

She polishes the willow pattern china
in a low cottage beside the motorway.
Soon there are cakes and tea before me,
photographs of a dead husband.
Outside the sun washes relentlessly
as the endless day grinds through the hours.
She danced to the wallpaper of family and history
but on a day like this the music stopped.

Now she observes from the terraces
routine events of the ordinary, waiting.
A tap drips at irregular intervals,
the green sink stain a unique signature.
A cat stretches to the chime of a clock.
Leaving, she runs after me with
a wild rose cut from the garden
to celebrate the silence we spent together.

NIGHT VISIT

Old women whisper their first love.
Men become boys in their mothers' arms.
The dog shivers a nightmare in his basket.
Ancestors framed over the fireplace,
gossip about the quality of furniture.

Graveyards glow on a distant hill.
The fox struts curiously between sheep.
A creak opens the cat's lazy eye.
Before a baby stretches for the breast,
the dark angel flies back into the west.

THE FENESTRATION HIGH TEA PARTY
for Paul Durcan

Where I come from we let houses do the talking.
They compare cleaners and crack up,
meet for sunlight and talk lawnmowers.
Don't mention septic tanks, one creaked
as she crossed her staircase,
percolation is where it's at.
We know who brushes your chimney, they settle
and order more insulation.
At the Ideal Housewives' Exhibition
I saw this woman, mortgage type, young.
Well, I waved my window boxes at her
but no deposit, she can plough my garden anytime.
Every house needs a man about the woman.
Old ladies like us on the right side of town
need to keep the grass cut and the paint fresh.
What about dry rot and property tax?
Oh, it's always the same after too much fibreglass.
Lighten up girls, show houses will never compete,
no fenestration, balustrades or winding avenues.
Here they come, home from work with kids in the dark.
We'd better shut up in case they have something to say.

A FLOCK OF ECHOES

Greetings from Galway,
the gold-chained mayor announced
to the refugees in the City Library,
before she quietly slipped away
to open a branch of Burger King.

He talked about his native lakes,
the snow-capped mountains
where ancestors reside,
where nobody owns land
and there are no fences.

We learned about the spirit of trees,
of being a mayor in Columbia
and the American Corporation.
He presented her with a flock of echoes
from the drowned valley.

Her secretary gave him a Guinness t-shirt,
but twinning is not on the agenda.
To this day nobody knows
why her alarm goes off
just as she is about to sleep.

THE ARRIVAL

When the dead man pursues you
along the side streets of reminiscence
it's useless to hide among a flock of students.
Run now for only he sees your negative,
which he will steal for his family album.

His mission is to shatter you
in an alley of yesterday's misfits
with his heart-shaped mirror.
Lure him into the meadows
where young women make idle talk,

where the confident May sunshine
will dazzle him with desire,
to prism it into colours
that will sacrifice him
on the altar of your arrival.

BUSHES
for Seamus Heaney

You were called to one side by wonder
before you could remember.
Catching moonbeams in a cot or talking to shadows.
An outsider now propelled into the world,
a schoolboy twisting toes into the softened tar alone.
You could walk across the border into perspective,
hover above yourself or walk onto the stage
to extract haulage from a line of empty conversation.
Your rowan today is indeed a lipsticked girl
waving outside my window off limits now
to my banal observations.
You took the weight bestowed
which many would have run from
and trusted that Larkin's empty pages would be filled.
And so they were, with the echoes of gates at milking time,
the slurp and sluice of bogwater under the skylark
decorating the sudden rush of blue sky with notes,
the blood and mud on your cousin's face on a country road.

You too would have chuckled at the circus following today
as the willows waved like pom-poms on your last journey.
Few of them would have seen the shine of the turned sod
or the old hawthorns, their berries hanging like ear rings
glowing as they are now
chosen on a whim by an evening sunshine
on a stony headland by a celestial torch
extinguishing as it creeps up the hills,
alerting us to seeing things just about now.
The way you wanted us to see
a perfect dénouement waiting for your absent fountain pen.

THE CONSPIRACY

When the respectable man finished the harvest
the glow of neon on the horizon beckoned.
He looked in the mirror at the cracks on his face,
said goodbye to the priest and the teacher.

At sunrise he abandoned the village.
After two days he descended into the city
where a woman linked him into a bar,
presenting him with four girls.

The next morning he went to the Museum,
the War Memorial, the National Gallery,
had high tea at the Royal Hotel
before limping home, poor but satiated.

The priest greeted the prodigal figure,
the city is a terrible place, he assured him.
Soon both men went separate ways
to empty houses, shaking their heads, laughing.

EMIGRATION

Most days I am a dry husk.
But today I seep into every crevice
down side streets, under delivery trucks
absolving the back entrances of nightclubs.

I overflow into cul-de-sacs,
soothe the cold perfection of fresh concrete,
comfort lonely cries in empty playgrounds,
until my tears leak into a steel gully.

Spilt, I creep home along the quays
wondering why they have to leave.
The blue night forgives me
as my three perfect drops flow into the ocean.

BETWEEN WARS

From nowhere, a day without pain.
Grateful, I kneel in the last pew
beside a scattering of old women,
the statues wait for the words we give them,
the angels want to drown us in peace.
This is how it must be after the armies retreat
and the dead are buried – the absence.

From the next street
echoes of children left behind
who have made a football from a pig's bladder
before the common misery begins,
before we hear the roar of the engines,
before our boys accept shiny uniforms
and the churches fill again with mothers.

THE INTIMATE DISTANCE

I often caught you dreaming on wet days.
Oh what I'd give now to know
all the roses this Indian man
is offering the dining couples,
but you knew how to break the connection
just before anything happened.

We hunkered under bushes,
waiting for the rain to clear
as they heaved under the squall.
We watched the horizon in vain
for a watery brightness
before the gulls swept in over a low wall
and we felt the shared silence
when the pools developed and merged.

Soon we would drive fat bullocks
through guttery gaps with a hazel stick
up a laneway where branches swayed,
pregnant with rotting haws
and stoic cattle dealers,
with dung-caked topcoats,
beat the frightened animals
into cosy winter sheds.

You'd have been proud of my journey,
the lengths I came to say goodbye,
the years lapsed, but never as far
as the intimate distance we shared,
letting you go now in a foreign city
under a sky we both could have read.

THE MOUNTAIN WOMAN

To understand north
she chose to live under the mountain
where the only company she had
was the echo of waterfalls,
where the twisted bushes
had forsaken the dank rocks.

In winter she clutched the summer
in home-made jams and apple pies,
she welcomed the storms with open arms
and begged them to blow through her,
when the snow flurried from the cirque
she consumed the absence in its wake.

In spring she knew the hour
when the sun emerged from the creek,
how to invite friends to share a bottle
and release the clot of distance
in rivulets of fresh thaw water.
She knew too when to gather the glasses.

THE OPEN ROAD

When some find a bicycle
they jump on, fall off a few times
before getting there, then they park it up
and consign it to the family museum.

Others learn to cycle at leisure,
take the scenic route, stopping at any excuse.
They arrive eventually.
It's the journey that counts they say.

Another group examines the chain, the spokes,
they dismantle it and reassemble it.
They agree that it may assist in the concept of travel
but suggest new brakes and lights.

Yet others pass it by without curiosity,
they know that at nightfall
it will make no difference when the noise starts
whether they have arrived or not.

UNAPPROVED ROAD
In memoriam Nuala O'Faolain

After the bell and before you crossed over
you spoke from the bottom of a well.
I abandoned the office and walked
to places where I gathered mushrooms,
to fairy forts, to the summit of drumlins,
to the edge of turloughs,
confettied myself with white-thorn blossom.
I sat on rocks, listened, inhaled.

That evening I walked through city streets
as rain sprinkled through a rainbow,
then sun splashed a mad light on fishing boats
and a cloud hung in anticipation.
You told us what we know, that this is all there is,
that we must stumble along the unapproved road,
and already I'm lonely for the light
of lost years reflected in remaining days.

WINTER GARDEN

Where my train stopped for no reason
a small boy ran towards me with a ball
from a perfect lawn, with a conservatory
picket fence all around, mom and dad smiling,
deciding where to plant an apple tree.

Outside, briars snared the fence.
The drunk looked to see if the shed was bolted.
A squall lifted a hayshed on the horizon.
A puny sun threw shadows from the meat factory.
From nowhere an empty goods train announced the night.

THE TRANSFER

I awake to a requiem for the desolate
being chanted outside my window
before dawn in a snowfield,
a spectre twisted in the moonlight
then faded into the bushes
where mother and my girlfriend
were drinking tea and reminiscing.

They smiled wistfully into the middle
distance as the morning sun spread,
a faint carpet under their feet.
He must have gone to school through the woods?
How did you know? My mother beamed.
You always know, she said, you always know.
My mother got up and walked away

WATERCOLOURS

Wild flowers drooping to the lakeshore,
students lay abandoned in long grasses,
only a breeze scars the mirror,
midge columns tangled in sunrays.

Leaves threshed off, glide to conclusion,
anxious swans display unease,
gathering sounds rumbling on the horizon,
cloud shadows stalking from the ocean.

Dark water swells into meadow drains,
hail storms lay siege to the island,
snow powder whispers through bothies,
foxes dream in the caverns of ancient burrows.

Crows appear on chimneys with sheep's wool,
roots heave through the concrete of forgotten towns,
catkins shiver in hope from a brittle sun,
the cuckoo announces another spring.

ROOM

Suddenly silence, except for Evelyn sobbing, sorry Master.
It was useless as he gave back her broken glasses,
his blue rage exorcised for that day.
We waited centuries for the bell,
time suspended as she gathered her torn copies,
watching the indifferent sunshine dapple the hills
the way it must have done a thousand years ago,
the way it does today, after that nothing could touch us.
All we wanted was some food and a roof.
People became another species.
We escaped to the ends of the earth,
we never left that room.

ONE DAY IN THE MEADOW

Grandfather and I heard the ringing.
He dropped the rake and left in a trance
without saying goodbye.
Soon a procession appeared
coming over the hill from the north
in single file, they followed the hooded man.

When they crossed the river
into our meadow, he shook the bell at me.
At least a hundred passed by,
nobody in my family saw them,
grandfather in his habit at the rear,
his hand outstretched to mine.

RAINY DAY IN CONNACHT

He listened to the shipping forecast late at night,
love-making had to wait –
Sole, Lundy, Fastnet, he was never at sea.
She wrapped herself in the comfort
of other people's storms.
When he cut the hay he settled the weather.

Napoleon could have used him on the Eastern Front,
D-Day was postponed by a man like him.
Now that he's gone I can tell his grandchildren
a bedtime story that a divorce referendum
was passed by a cold front –
raining all that long day in Connacht.

PROCESSION

One morning the street was empty
except for a sound like distant thunder.
Slowly they came into view
like the distillation of premonition,
with blood running from their drums
in a slow march towards the church of peace,
the women in black carrying the virgin,
the boys playing the trumpets of righteousness.

An Indian girl shivered in the sunshine
as the ghost of Spanish history ran past.
They receded, washing the streets with morality,
after them a clot of tourists and the street sweeper,
then someone pulling a cart of beer and beans
before the day spread out its secular mantel,
a playground for every living thing.

THAT OFFICE LIGHT

After five it throws itself across desks and computers,
over half-drunk mugs of coffee that say Salou Uncut,
creeps along postcards from the Canaries
beside last year's Christmas party photos.
Then it suddenly discovers the inside office for a while
before the factory shadow crawls over the copier,
the shelves marked 'Mayo 2000 And Beyond' and the file
'Proposed Sewage Treatment Plant for Kilmaine'.
The cleaner knows she must bring her work to the door
where the light now rests on the glass, and leaves
only a triangle retreating palpably up the wall.

Something is happening in the far office and it is spreading.
Soon there's only a hint of a distant sunray on a far hill.
The in-trays wait, a door closes, a light has come
on in the clerk's office, a water tank is filling.
The sound of the caretaker's key shatters
as squinting new light cuts confident angles
of a new day into the mission statement.
He checks every office, relieved.
The girls colonise but never know
who moved the invoices to the out-tray,
Ibiza now only twenty three days away.

THE POLISHED ARROW

Early summer, warm breeze
wafting from the park
laden with little gusts of sudden blossom essence.
Late sunshine on red brick,
a thunderstorm grumbling on the horizon,
girls heavy-eyed with purpose out for the night,
a plane winking towards the airport.
Then without warning I am stumbling
into the thickening air,
gulping awareness like a whale hoovering krill.

Then it happens like a blue Atlantic sky
arriving on the horizon,
I suddenly love everybody and everything.
It occurs to me
I could live like this, never looking back,
peddling each new day into fresh discovery
like a raw vulnerable thing,
striving like a polished arrow
flung towards the moon
in search of some ultimate truth.